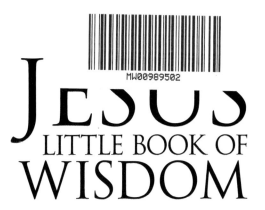

JESUS
LITTLE BOOK OF
WISDOM

HarperCollins*Publishers*
1 London Bridge Street
London SE1 9GF
www.harpercollins.co.uk

First published by HarperCollins*Publishers* in 2017

1 3 5 7 9 10 8 6 4 2

Compiled by Andrea Kirk Assaf
Scripture quotations are from New Revised Standard Version Bible, copyright
© 1989 National Council of the Churches of Christ in the United States of
America. Used by permission. All rights reserved worldwide.
Cover design by e-Digital Design
Cover photo credit: The Christ Pantocrator of the Deesis mosaic (13th-century) in Hagia
Sophia (Istanbul, Turkey). Photo by Myrabella / Wikimedia Commons / CC BY-SA 3.0
Text design by e-Digital Design

A catalogue record for this book is available from the British Library

ISBN 978-0-00-826224-2

Printed and bound in China by RR Donnelley Asia Print Solutions.

MIX

Paper from responsible sources

FSC™ C007454

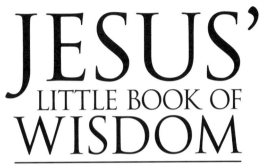

JESUS'
LITTLE BOOK OF
WISDOM

Guidance, Hope and Comfort
for Every Day

Compiled by Andrea Kirk Assaf

WILLIAM
COLLINS

But strive first for the kingdom of God and his righteousness, and all these things will be given to you as well.

Matthew 6:33

Contents

A Note from the Compiler

Oftentimes readers of books of quotations will open a collection at random, seeking to be surprised by or led to a word of advice. Sometimes a reader will go through the entire work in order, from beginning to end. And other readers choose quotes according to themes of particular interest. This collection of quotes, all taken from the New Revised Standard Version Bible, was put together with all three types of readers in mind.

While the quotes can offer food for thought on their own, the Scriptural source is cited for each one, allowing readers to further research the context surrounding Jesus' words for those selecting quotes at random. For the reader interested in themes or reading the work from start to finish, the book's themes were selected and arranged in their particular order to mirror the journey of one who seeks to form a relationship with Jesus through His words.

The journey of a Christian begins with the initial *call to discipleship*, then matures through the practices of *listening, watching, and remembering* Christ's admonitions and promises.

The Christian can also be sure of partaking in Jesus' *trials and tribulations*, as well as receiving His *consolation and comfort*. When the Christian chooses the path of *repentance and forgiveness*, it becomes possible to recognize and experience *grace and sanctification*. The entire journey all rests upon *faith and fulfillment* of Christ's promises to those who listen to His word and follow His call. May this little book accompany you on your journey and God speed!

Andrea Kirk Assaf
Holy Week 2017
Remus, Michigan

PART ONE

The Call to Discipleship

I give you a new commandment, that you love one another. Just as I have loved you, you also should love one another. By this everyone will know that you are my disciples, if you have love for one another.

John 13:34–35

Whoever is faithful in a very little is faithful also in much; and whoever is dishonest in a very little is dishonest also in much. If then you have not been faithful with the dishonest wealth, who will entrust to you the true riches? And if you have not been faithful with what belongs to another, who will give you what is your own? No slave can serve two masters; for a slave will either hate the one and love the other, or be devoted to the one and despise the other. You cannot serve God and wealth.

Luke 16:10–13

I do not call you servants any longer, because the servant does not know what the master is doing; but I have called you friends, because I have made known to you everything that I have heard from my Father. You did not choose me but I chose you. And I appointed you to go and bear fruit, fruit that will last, so that the Father will give you whatever you ask him in my name. I am giving you these commands so that you may love one another.

John 15:15–17

I am the true vine, and my Father is the vinegrower. He removes every branch in me that bears no fruit. Every branch that bears fruit He prunes to make it bear more fruit. You have already been cleansed by the word that I have spoken to you. Abide in me as I abide in you. Just as the branch cannot bear fruit by itself unless it abides in the vine, neither can you unless you abide in me. I am the vine, you are the branches. Those who abide in me and I in them bear much fruit, because apart from me you can do nothing. Whoever does not abide in me is thrown away like a branch and withers; such branches are gathered, thrown into the fire, and burned. If you abide in me, and my words abide in you, ask for whatever you wish, and it will be done for you. My Father is glorified by this, that you bear much fruit and become my disciples.

John 15:1–8

Whoever is not with me is against me, and whoever does not gather with me scatters.

Luke 11:23

Truly I tell you, there is no one who has left house or wife or brothers or parents or children, for the sake of the kingdom of God, who will not get back very much more in this age, and in the age to come eternal life.

Luke 18:29–30

If you continue in my word, you are truly my disciples; and you will know the truth, and the truth will make you free.

John 8:31–32

Whoever does the will of God is my brother and sister and mother.

Mark 3:35

While he was saying this, a woman in the crowd raised her voice and said to him, "Blessed is the womb that bore you and the breasts that nursed you!" But he said, "Blessed rather are those who hear the word of God and obey it!"

Luke 11:27–28

As he walked by the Sea of Galilee, he saw two brothers, Simon, who is called Peter, and Andrew his brother, casting a net into the sea—for they were fishermen. And he said to them, "Follow me, and I will make you fish for people." Immediately they left their nets and followed him.

Matthew 4:18–20

Whoever serves me must follow me, and where I am, there will my servant be also. Whoever serves me, the Father will honor.

John 12:26

Those who speak on their own seek their own glory; but the one who seeks the glory of him who sent him is true, and there is nothing false in him.

John 7:18

Do you not say, "Four months more, then comes the harvest"? But I tell you, look around you, and see how the fields are ripe for harvesting. The reaper is already receiving wages and is gathering fruit for eternal life, so that sower and reaper may rejoice together. For here the saying holds true, "One sows and another reaps." I sent you to reap that for which you did not labor. Others have labored, and you have entered into their labor.

John 4:35–38

If any want to become my followers, let them deny themselves and take up their cross and follow me. For those who want to save their life will lose it, and those who lose their life for my sake, and for the sake of the gospel, will save it.

Mark 8:34–35

It is written in the prophets, "And they shall all be taught by God." Everyone who has heard and learned from the Father comes to me.

John 6:45

For what will it profit them to gain the whole world and forfeit their life? Indeed, what can they give in return for their life?

Mark 8:36–37

After he had washed their feet, had put on his robe, and had returned to the table, he said to them, "Do you know what I have done to you? You call me Teacher and Lord— and you are right, for that is what I am. So if I, your Lord and Teacher, have washed your feet, you also ought to wash one another's feet. For

I have set you an example, that you also should do as I have done to you. Very truly, I tell you, servants are not greater than their master, nor are messengers greater than the one who sent them. If you know these things, you are blessed if you do them."

John 13:12–17

In all this I have given you an example that by such work we must support the weak, remembering the words of the Lord Jesus, for he himself said, "It is more blessed to give than to receive."

Acts 20:35

Are there not twelve hours of daylight? Those who walk during the day do not stumble, because they see the light of this world. But those who walk at night stumble, because the light is not in them.

John 11:9–10

Whoever wants to be first must be last of all and servant of all.

Mark 9:35

Whoever is not against us is for us. For truly I tell you, whoever gives you a cup of water to drink because you bear the name of Christ will by no means lose the reward.

Mark 9:40–41

Very truly, I tell you, whoever receives one whom I send receives me; and whoever receives me receives Him who sent me.

John 13:20

"Let the little children come to me; do not stop them; for it is to such as these that the kingdom of God belongs. Truly I tell you, whoever does not receive the kingdom of God as a little child will never enter it." And he took them up in his arms, laid his hands on them, and blessed them.

Mark 10:14–16

Jesus, looking at him, loved him and said,
"You lack one thing; go, sell what you own,
and give the money to the poor, and you will
have treasure in heaven; then come, follow me."

Mark 10:21

You know that among the Gentiles those whom they recognize as their rulers lord it over them, and their great ones are tyrants over them. But it is not so among you; but whoever wishes to become great among you must be your servant, and whoever wishes to be first among you must be slave of all.

Mark 10:42–44

And whenever you pray, do not be like the hypocrites; for they love to stand and pray in the synagogues and at the street corners, so that they may be seen by others. Truly I tell you, they have received their reward. But whenever you pray, go into your room and shut the door and pray to your Father who is in secret; and your Father who sees in secret will reward you.

Matthew 6:5–6

And whenever you fast, do not look dismal, like the hypocrites, for they disfigure their faces so as to show others that they are fasting. Truly I tell you, they have received their reward. But when you fast, put oil on your head and wash your face, so that your fasting may be seen not by others but by your Father who is in secret; and your Father who sees in secret will reward you.

Matthew 6:16–18

In everything do to others as you would have them do to you; for this is the law and the prophets.

Matthew 7:12

The harvest is plentiful, but the laborers are few; therefore ask the Lord of the harvest to send out laborers into his harvest.

Matthew 9:37–38

I am sending you out like sheep into the midst of wolves; so be wise as serpents and innocent as doves.

Matthew 10:16

A disciple is not above the teacher, nor a slave above the master; it is enough for the disciple to be like the teacher, and the slave like the master.

Matthew 10:25

Whoever gives even a cup of cold water to one of these little ones in the name of a disciple—truly I tell you, none of these will lose their reward.

Matthew 10:42

But blessed are your eyes, for they see, and your ears, for they hear. Truly I tell you, many prophets and righteous people longed to see what you see, but did not see it, and to hear what you hear, but did not hear it.

Matthew 13:16–17

Therefore every scribe who has been trained for the kingdom of heaven is like the master of a household who brings out of his treasure what is new and what is old.

Matthew 13:52

Go therefore and make disciples of all nations, baptizing them in the name of the Father and of the Son and of the Holy Spirit, and teaching them to obey everything that I have commanded you.

Matthew 28:19–20

As they were going along the road, someone said to him, "I will follow you wherever you go." And Jesus said to him, "Foxes have holes, and birds of the air have nests; but the Son of Man has nowhere to lay his head." To another he said, "Follow me." But he said, "Lord, first let me go and bury my father." But Jesus said to him, "Let the dead bury their own dead; but as for you, go and proclaim the kingdom of God." Another said, "I will follow you, Lord; but let me first say farewell to those at my home." Jesus said to him, "No one who puts a hand to the plow and looks back is fit for the kingdom of God."

Luke 9:57–62

Whoever comes to me and does not hate father and mother, wife and children, brothers and sisters, yes, and even life itself, cannot be my disciple.

Luke 14:26

Whoever does not carry the cross and follow me cannot be my disciple.

Luke 14:27

For which of you, intending to build a tower, does not first sit down and estimate the cost, to see whether he has enough to complete it? Otherwise, when he has laid a foundation and is not able to finish, all who see it will begin to ridicule him, saying, "This fellow began to build and was not able to finish." Or what king, going out to wage war against another king, will not sit down first and consider whether he is able with ten thousand to oppose the one who comes against him with twenty thousand? If he cannot, then, while the other is still far away, he sends a delegation and asks for the terms of peace. So therefore, none of you can become my disciple if you do not give up all your possessions.

Luke 14:28–33

PART TWO

Listen, Watch, Remember

Listen! I am standing at the door, knocking; if you hear my voice and open the door, I will come in to you and eat with you, and you with me.

Revelation 3:20

You say that I am a king. For this I was born, and for this I came into the world, to testify to the truth. Everyone who belongs to the truth listens to my voice.

John 18:37

This is my commandment, that you love one another as I have loved you. No one has greater love than this, to lay down one's life for one's friends. You are my friends if you do what I command you.

John 15:12–14

And he said to them, "Take care! Be on your guard against all kinds of greed; for one's life does not consist in the abundance of possessions."

Luke 12:15

Be on guard so that your hearts are not weighed down with dissipation and drunkenness and the worries of this life …

Luke 21:34

Be alert at all times, praying that you may have the strength to escape all these things that will take place, and to stand before the Son of Man.

Luke 21:36

The light is with you for a little longer. Walk while you have the light, so that the darkness may not overtake you. If you walk in the darkness, you do not know where you are going. While you have the light, believe in the light, so that you may become children of light.

John 12:35–36

Very truly, I tell you, anyone who does not enter the sheepfold by the gate but climbs in by another way is a thief and a bandit. The one who enters by the gate is the shepherd of the sheep. The gatekeeper opens the gate for him, and the sheep hear his voice. He calls his own sheep by name and leads them out. When he has brought out all his own, he goes ahead of them, and the sheep follow him because they know his voice. They will not follow a stranger, but they will run from him because they do not know the voice of strangers.

John 10:1–5

Do you still not perceive or understand? Are your hearts hardened? Do you have eyes, and fail to see? Do you have ears, and fail to hear? And do you not remember?

Mark 8:17–18

We must work the works of him who sent me while it is day; night is coming when no one can work.

John 9:4

I know your works; you have a name of being alive, but you are dead. Wake up, and strengthen what remains and is on the point of death, for I have not found your works perfect in the sight of my God. Remember then what you received and heard; obey it, and repent. If you do not wake up, I will come like a thief, and you will not know at what hour I will come to you.

Revelation 3:1–3

Do not work for the food that perishes, but for the food that endures for eternal life, which the Son of Man will give you. For it is on him that God the Father has set his seal.

John 6:27

No one sews a piece of unshrunk cloth on an old cloak; otherwise, the patch pulls away from it, the new from the old, and a worse tear is made. And no one puts new wine into old wineskins; otherwise, the wine will burst the skins, and the wine is lost, and so are the skins; but one puts new wine into fresh wineskins.

Mark 2:21–22

They who have my commandments and keep them are those who love me; and those who love me will be loved by my Father, and I will love them and reveal myself to them.

John 14:21

If a kingdom is divided against itself, that kingdom cannot stand. And if a house is divided against itself, that house will not be able to stand.

Mark 3:24–25

I have said these things to you while I am still with you. But the Advocate, the Holy Spirit, whom the Father will send in my name, will teach you everything, and remind you of all that I have said to you.

John 14:25–26

Pay attention to what you hear; the measure you give will be the measure you get, and still more will be given you. For to those who have, more will be given; and from those who have nothing, even what they have will be taken away.

Mark 4:24–25

He said to them, "Isaiah prophesied rightly about you hypocrites, as it is written, 'This people honors me with their lips, but their hearts are far from me; in vain do they worship me, teaching human precepts as doctrines.' You abandon the commandment of God and hold to human tradition."

Mark 7:6–8

If you conquer, you will be clothed like them in white robes, and I will not blot your name out of the book of life; I will confess your name before my Father and before his angels.

Revelation 3:5

You are the salt of the earth; but if salt has lost its taste, how can its saltiness be restored? It is no longer good for anything, but is thrown out and trampled underfoot.

Matthew 5:13

No one after lighting a lamp puts it under the bushel basket, but on the lampstand, and it gives light to all in the house. In the same way, let your light shine before others, so that they may see your good works and give glory to your Father in heaven.

Matthew 5:15–16

If you love me, you will keep my commandments. And I will ask the Father, and He will give you another Advocate, to be with you forever. This is the Spirit of truth, whom the world cannot receive, because it neither sees him nor knows him. You know him, because he abides with you, and he will be in you.

John 14:15–17

Therefore, whoever breaks one of the least of these commandments, and teaches others to do the same, will be called least in the kingdom of heaven; but whoever does them and teaches them will be called great in the kingdom of heaven. For I tell you, unless your righteousness exceeds that of the scribes and Pharisees, you will never enter the kingdom of heaven.

Matthew 5:19–20

If any of you put a stumbling block before one of these little ones who believe in me, it would be better for you if a great millstone were hung around your neck and you were thrown into the sea.

Mark 9:42

Salt is good; but if salt has lost its saltiness, how can you season it? Have salt in yourselves, and be at peace with one another.

Mark 9:50

Again, you have heard that it was said to those of ancient times, "You shall not swear falsely, but carry out the vows you have made to the Lord." But I say to you, Do not swear at all, either by heaven, for it is the throne of God, or by the earth, for it is His footstool, or by Jerusalem, for it is the city of the great King. And do not swear by your head, for you cannot make one hair white or black. Let your word be "Yes, Yes" or "No, No"; anything more than this comes from the evil one.

Matthew 5:33–37

Give to everyone who begs from you, and do not refuse anyone who wants to borrow from you.

Matthew 5:42

Beware of practicing your piety before others in order to be seen by them; for then you have no reward from your Father in heaven. So whenever you give alms, do not sound a trumpet before you, as the hypocrites do in the synagogues and in the streets, so that they may be praised by others. Truly I tell you, they have received their reward. But when you give alms, do not let your left hand know what your right hand is doing, so that your alms may be done in secret; and your Father who sees in secret will reward you.

Matthew 6:1–4

Do not store up for yourselves treasures on earth, where moth and rust consume and where thieves break in and steal; but store up for yourselves treasures in heaven, where neither moth nor rust consumes and where thieves do not break in and steal. For where your treasure is, there your heart will be also.

Matthew 6:19–21

Beware that no one leads you astray. Many will come in my name and say, "I am he!" and they will lead many astray.

Mark 13:5–6

The eye is the lamp of the body. So, if your eye is healthy, your whole body will be full of light; but if your eye is unhealthy, your whole body will be full of darkness. If then the light in you is darkness, how great is the darkness!

Matthew 6:22–23

No one can serve two masters; for a slave will either hate the one and love the other, or be devoted to the one and despise the other. You cannot serve God and wealth.

Matthew 6:24

But about that day or hour no one knows, neither the angels in heaven, nor the Son, but only the Father. Beware, keep alert; for you do not know when the time will come. It is like a man going on a journey, when he leaves home and puts his slaves in charge, each with his work, and commands the doorkeeper to be on the watch. Therefore, keep awake—for you do not know when the master of the house will come, in the evening, or at midnight, or at cockcrow, or at dawn, or else he may find you asleep when he comes suddenly. And what I say to you I say to all: "Keep awake."

Mark 13:32–37

As the Father has loved me, so I have loved you; abide in my love. If you keep my commandments, you will abide in my love, just as I have kept my Father's commandments and abide in His love. I have said these things to you so that my joy may be in you, and that your joy may be complete.

John 15:9–11

Beware of false prophets, who come to you in sheep's clothing but inwardly are ravenous wolves. You will know them by their fruits. Are grapes gathered from thorns, or figs from thistles? In the same way, every good tree bears good fruit, but the bad tree bears bad fruit. A good tree cannot bear bad fruit, nor can a bad tree bear good fruit. Every tree that does not bear good fruit is cut down and thrown into the fire. Thus you will know them by their fruits.

Matthew 7:15–20

Everyone then who hears these words of mine and acts on them will be like a wise man who built his house on rock. The rain fell, the floods came, and the winds blew and beat on that house, but it did not fall, because it had been founded on rock. And everyone who hears these words of mine and does not act on them will be like a foolish man who built his house on sand. The rain fell, and the floods came, and the winds blew and beat against that house, and it fell—and great was its fall!

Matthew 7:24–29

He said to him, "'You shall love the Lord your God with all your heart, and with all your soul, and with all your mind.' This is the greatest and first commandment. And a second is like it: 'You shall love your neighbor as yourself.' On these two commandments hang all the law and the prophets."

Matthew 22:37–40

Then the kingdom of heaven will be like this. Ten bridesmaids took their lamps and went to meet the bridegroom. Five of them were foolish, and five were wise. When the foolish took their lamps, they took no oil with them; but the wise took flasks of oil with their lamps. As the bridegroom was delayed, all of them became drowsy and slept. But at midnight there was a shout, "Look! Here is the bridegroom! Come out to meet him." Then all those bridesmaids got up and trimmed their lamps. The foolish said to the wise, "Give us some of your oil, for our lamps are going out." But the wise replied, "No! there will not be enough for you and for us; you had better go to the dealers and buy some for yourselves." And while they went to buy it, the bridegroom came, and those who were ready went with him into the wedding banquet; and the door was shut. Later the other bridesmaids came also, saying, "Lord, lord, open to us." But he replied, "Truly I tell you, I do not know you." Keep awake therefore, for you know neither the day nor the hour.

Matthew 25:1–13

To what then will I compare the people of this generation, and what are they like? They are like children sitting in the marketplace and calling to one another, "We played the flute for you, and you did not dance; we wailed, and you did not weep."

Luke 7:31–32

Wisdom is vindicated by all her children.

Luke 7:35

Be dressed for action and have your lamps lit; be like those who are waiting for their master to return from the wedding banquet, so that they may open the door for him as soon as he comes and knocks. Blessed are those slaves whom the master finds alert when he comes; truly I tell you, he will fasten his belt and have them sit down to eat, and he will come and serve them. If he comes during the middle of the night, or near dawn, and finds them so, blessed are those slaves.

But know this: if the owner of the house had known at what hour the thief was coming, he would not have let his house be broken into. You also must be ready, for the Son of Man is coming at an unexpected hour.

Luke 12:35–40

Then pay attention to how you listen; for to those who have, more will be given; and from those who do not have, even what they seem to have will be taken away.

Luke 8:18

PART THREE

Trial and Tribulation

Very truly, I tell you, you will weep and mourn, but the world will rejoice; you will have pain, but your pain will turn into joy. When a woman is in labor, she has pain, because her hour has come. But when her child is born, she no longer remembers the anguish because of the joy of having brought a human being into the world. So you have pain now; but I will see you again, and your hearts will rejoice, and no one will take your joy from you.

John 16:20–22

Then the devil took him to the holy city and placed him on the pinnacle of the temple, saying to him, "If you are the Son of God, throw yourself down; for it is written, 'He will command his angels concerning you,' and 'On their hands they will bear you up, so that you will not dash your foot against a stone.'" Jesus said to him, "Again it is written, 'Do not put the Lord your God to the test.'"

Matthew 4:5–7

From everyone to whom much has been given, much will be required; and from the one to whom much has been entrusted, even more will be demanded.

Luke 12:48

If the world hates you, be aware that it hated me before it hated you. If you belonged to the world, the world would love you as its own. Because you do not belong to the world, but I have chosen you out of the world—therefore the world hates you. Remember the word that I said to you, "Servants are not greater than their master." If they persecuted me, they will persecute you; if they kept my word, they will keep yours also. But they will do all these things to you on account of my name, because they do not know him who sent me. If I had not come and spoken to them, they would not have sin; but now they have no excuse for their sin. Whoever hates me hates my Father also. If I had not done among them the works that no one else did, they would not have sin. But now they have seen and hated both me and my Father. It was to fulfill the word that is written in their law, "They hated me without a cause."

John 15:18–25

Simon, Simon, listen! Satan has demanded to sift all of you like wheat, but I have prayed for you that your own faith may not fail; and you, when once you have turned back, strengthen your brothers.

Luke 22:31–32

Pray that you may not come into the time of trial.

Luke 22:40

Father, if you are willing, remove this cup from me; yet, not my will but yours be done. Then an angel from heaven appeared to him and gave him strength. In his anguish he prayed more earnestly, and his sweat became like great drops of blood falling down on the ground.

Luke 22:42–44

Now my soul is troubled. And what should I say—"Father, save me from this hour"? No, it is for this reason that I have come to this hour.

John 12:27

In a certain city there was a judge who neither feared God nor had respect for people. In that city there was a widow who kept coming to him and saying, "Grant me justice against my opponent." For a while he refused; but later he said to himself, "Though I have no fear of God and no respect for anyone, yet because this widow keeps bothering me, I will grant her justice, so that she may not wear me out by continually coming." And the Lord said, "Listen to what the unjust judge says." And will not God grant justice to his chosen ones who cry to him day and night? Will he delay long in helping them? I tell you, he will quickly grant justice to them.

Luke 18:2–8

You will be hated by all because of my name. But not a hair of your head will perish. By your endurance you will gain your souls.

Luke 21:17–19

Then he began to teach them that the Son of Man must undergo great suffering, and be rejected by the elders, the chief priests, and the scribes, and be killed, and after three days rise again. He said all this quite openly. And Peter took him aside and began to rebuke him. But turning and looking at his disciples, he rebuked Peter and said, "Get behind me, Satan! For you are setting your mind not on divine things but on human things."

Mark 8:31–33

Blessed are those who are persecuted for righteousness' sake, for theirs is the kingdom of heaven.

Matthew 5:10

Blessed are you when people revile you and persecute you and utter all kinds of evil against you falsely on my account.

Matthew 5:11

Again, the devil took him to a very high mountain and showed him all the kingdoms of the world and their splendor; and he said to him, "All these I will give you, if you will fall down and worship me." Jesus said to him, "Away with you, Satan! for it is written, 'Worship the Lord your God, and serve only him.'"

Matthew 4:8–10

When they bring you to trial and hand you over, do not worry beforehand about what you are to say; but say whatever is given you at that time, for it is not you who speak, but the Holy Spirit.

Mark 13:11

And you will be hated by all because of my name. But the one who endures to the end will be saved.

Mark 13:13

He said, "Abba, Father, for you all things are possible; remove this cup from me; yet, not what I want, but what you want."

Mark 14:36

He came and found them sleeping; and he said to Peter, "Simon, are you asleep? Could you not keep awake one hour? Keep awake and pray that you may not come into the time of trial; the spirit indeed is willing, but the flesh is weak."

Mark 14:37–38

Jesus cried out with a loud voice, "Eloi, Eloi, lema sabachthani?" which means, "My God, my God, why have you forsaken me?"

Mark 15:34

Now as they went on their way, he entered a certain village, where a woman named Martha welcomed him into her home. She had a sister named Mary, who sat at the Lord's feet and listened to what he was saying. But Martha was distracted by her many tasks; so she came to him and asked, "Lord, do you not care that my sister has left me to do all the work by myself? Tell her then to help me." But the Lord answered her, "Martha, Martha, you are worried and distracted by many things; there is need of only one thing. Mary has chosen the better part, which will not be taken away from her."

Luke 10:38–42

Enter through the narrow gate; for the gate is wide and the road is easy that leads to destruction, and there are many who take it. For the gate is narrow and the road is hard that leads to life, and there are few who find it.

Matthew 7:13–14

My Father, if this cannot pass unless I drink it, your will be done.

Matthew 26:42

PART FOUR

Repentance and Forgiveness

I reprove and discipline those whom I love. Be earnest, therefore, and repent.

Revelation 3:19

You judge by human standards; I judge no one. Yet even if I do judge, my judgment is valid; for it is not I alone who judge, but I and the Father who sent me.

John 8:15–16

Do not sin any more, so that nothing worse happens to you.

John 5:14

So he said to them, "You are those who justify yourselves in the sight of others; but God knows your hearts; for what is prized by human beings is an abomination in the sight of God."

Luke 16:15

For the Son of Man came to seek out and to save the lost.

Luke 19:10

Jesus said to them again, "Peace be with you. As the Father has sent me, so I send you." When he had said this, he breathed on them and said to them, "Receive the Holy Spirit. If you forgive the sins of any, they are forgiven them; if you retain the sins of any, they are retained."

John 20:21–23

There was a rich man who was dressed in purple and fine linen and who feasted sumptuously every day. And at his gate lay a poor man named Lazarus, covered with sores, who longed to satisfy his hunger with what fell from the rich man's table; even the dogs would come and lick his sores. The poor man died and was carried away by the angels to be with Abraham. The rich man also died and was buried. In Hades, where he was being tormented, he looked up and saw Abraham far away with Lazarus by his side. He called out,

"Father Abraham, have mercy on me, and send Lazarus to dip the tip of his finger in water and cool my tongue; for I am in agony in these flames." But Abraham said, "Child, remember that during your lifetime you received your good things, and Lazarus in like manner evil things; but now he is comforted here, and you are in agony. Besides all this, between you and us a great chasm has been fixed, so that those who might want to pass from here to you cannot do so, and no one can cross from there to us." He said, "Then, father, I beg you to send him to my father's house—for I have five brothers—that he may warn them, so that they will not also come into this place of torment." Abraham replied, "They have Moses and the prophets; they should listen to them." He said, "No, father Abraham; but if someone goes to them from the dead, they will repent." He said to him, "If they do not listen to Moses and the prophets, neither will they be convinced even if someone rises from the dead."

Luke 16:19–31

If another disciple sins, you must rebuke the offender, and if there is repentance, you must forgive. And if the same person sins against you seven times a day, and turns back to you seven times and says, "I repent," you must forgive.

Luke 17:3–4

Let anyone among you who is without sin be the first to throw a stone at her.

John 8:7

Is a lamp brought in to be put under the bushel basket, or under the bed, and not on the lampstand? For there is nothing hidden, except to be disclosed; nor is anything secret, except to come to light.

Mark 4:21–22

Do not judge by appearances, but judge with right judgment.

John 7:24

Jesus answered them, "Very truly, I tell you, you are looking for me, not because you saw signs, but because you ate your fill of the loaves."

John 6: 26

I know your works; you are neither cold nor hot. I wish that you were either cold or hot.

Revelation 3:15

Those who are well have no need of a physician, but those who are sick; I have come to call not the righteous but sinners.

Mark 2:17

From that time Jesus began to proclaim, "Repent, for the kingdom of heaven has come near."

Matthew 4:17

B lessed are the merciful, for they will receive mercy.

Matthew 5:7

It is what comes out of a person that defiles. For it is from within, from the human heart, that evil intentions come: fornication, theft, murder, adultery, avarice, wickedness, deceit, licentiousness, envy, slander, pride, folly. All these evil things come from within, and they defile a person.

Mark 7:20–23

Do not complain among yourselves.

John 6:43

For you say, "I am rich, I have prospered, and I need nothing." You do not realize that you are wretched, pitiable, poor, blind, and naked. Therefore I counsel you to buy from me gold refined by fire so that you may be rich; and white robes to clothe you and to keep the shame of your nakedness from being seen; and salve to anoint your eyes so that you may see.

Revelation 3:17–18

You have heard that it was said to those of ancient times, "You shall not murder"; and "whoever murders shall be liable to judgment." But I say to you that if you are angry with a brother or sister, you will be liable to judgment; and if you insult a brother or sister, you will be liable to the council; and if you say, "You fool," you will be liable to the hell of fire. So when you are offering your gift at the altar, if you remember that your brother or sister has something against you, leave your gift there before the altar and go; first be reconciled to your brother or sister, and then come and offer your gift.

Matthew 5:21–24

Blessed are the peacemakers, for they will be called children of God.

Matthew 5:9

Come to terms quickly with your accuser while you are on the way to court with him, or your accuser may hand you over to the judge, and the judge to the guard, and you will be thrown into prison. Truly I tell you, you will never get out until you have paid the last penny.

Matthew 5:25–26

If your hand causes you to stumble, cut it off; it is better for you to enter life maimed than to have two hands and to go to hell, to the unquenchable fire. And if your foot causes you to stumble, cut it off; it is better for you to enter life lame than to have two feet and to be thrown into hell. And if your eye causes you to stumble, tear it out; it is better for you to enter the kingdom of God with one eye than to have two eyes and to be thrown into hell, where their worm never dies, and the fire is never quenched.

Mark 9:43–48

If your right eye causes you to sin, tear it out and throw it away; it is better for you to lose one of your members than for your whole body to be thrown into hell. And if your right hand causes you to sin, cut it off and throw it away; it is better for you to lose one of your members than for your whole body to go into hell.

Matthew 5:29–30

You have heard that it was said, "You shall love your neighbor and hate your enemy." But I say to you, Love your enemies and pray for those who persecute you, so that you may be children of your Father in heaven; for he makes his sun rise on the evil and on the good, and sends rain on the righteous and on the unrighteous. For if you love those who love you, what reward do you have? Do not even the tax collectors do the same? And if you greet only your brothers and sisters, what more are you doing than others? Do not even the Gentiles do the same?

Matthew 5:43–47

You have heard that it was said, "An eye for an eye and a tooth for a tooth." But I say to you, Do not resist an evildoer. But if anyone strikes you on the right cheek, turn the other also; and if anyone wants to sue you and take your coat, give your cloak as well; and if anyone forces you to go one mile, go also the second mile.

Matthew 5:38–41

Whenever you stand praying, forgive, if you have anything against anyone; so that your Father in heaven may also forgive you your trespasses.

Mark 11:25

A man planted a vineyard, put a fence around it, dug a pit for the wine press, and built a watchtower; then he leased it to tenants and went to another country. When the season came, he sent a slave to the tenants to collect from them his share of the produce of the vineyard. But they seized him, and beat him, and sent him away empty-handed. And again he sent another slave to them; this one they beat over the head and insulted. Then he sent another, and that one they killed. And so it was with many others; some they beat, and others they killed. He had still one other, a beloved son. Finally he sent him to them, saying, "They will respect my son." But those tenants said to one another, "This is the heir; come, let us kill him, and the inheritance will be ours." So they seized him, killed him, and threw him out of the vineyard. What then will the owner of the vineyard do? He will come and destroy the tenants and give the vineyard to others.

Mark 12:1–9

For if you forgive others their trespasses, your heavenly Father will also forgive you; but if you do not forgive others, neither will your Father forgive your trespasses.

Matthew 6:14–15

Beware of the scribes, who like to walk around in long robes, and to be greeted with respect in the marketplaces, and to have the best seats in the synagogues and places of honor at banquets! They devour widows' houses and for the sake of appearance say long prayers. They will receive the greater condemnation.

Mark 12:38–40

Do not judge, so that you may not be judged. For with the judgment you make you will be judged, and the measure you give will be the measure you get.

Matthew 7:1–2

Why do you see the speck in your neighbor's eye, but do not notice the log in your own eye? Or how can you say to your neighbor, "Let me take the speck out of your eye," while the log is in your own eye? You hypocrite, first take the log out of your own eye, and then you will see clearly to take the speck out of your neighbor's eye.

Matthew 7:3–5

Either make the tree good, and its fruit good; or make the tree bad, and its fruit bad; for the tree is known by its fruit. You brood of vipers! How can you speak good things, when you are evil? For out of the abundance of the heart the mouth speaks. The good person brings good things out of a good treasure, and the evil person brings evil things out of an evil treasure. I tell you, on the day of judgment you will have to give an account for every careless word you utter; for by your words you will be justified, and by your words you will be condemned.

Matthew 12:33–37

Jesus spoke up and said to him, "Simon, I have something to say to you." "Teacher," he replied, "speak." "A certain creditor had two debtors; one owed five hundred denarii, and the other fifty. When they could not pay, he canceled the debts for both of them. Now which of them will love him more?" Simon answered, "I suppose the one for whom he canceled the greater debt." And Jesus said to him, "You have judged rightly." Then turning toward the woman, he said to Simon, "Do you see this woman? I entered your house; you gave me no water for my feet, but she has bathed my feet with her tears and dried them with her hair. You gave me no kiss, but from the time I came in she has not stopped kissing my feet. You did not anoint my head with oil, but she has anointed my feet with ointment. Therefore, I tell you, her sins, which were many, have been forgiven; hence she has shown great love. But the one to whom little is forgiven, loves little." Then he said to her, "Your sins are forgiven." But those who were at the table with him began to say among themselves, "Who is this who even forgives sins?" And he said to the woman, "Your faith has saved you; go in peace."

Luke 7:40–50

Neither do I condemn you. Go your way, and from now on do not sin again.

John 8:11

Every plant that my heavenly Father has not planted will be uprooted.

Matthew 15:13

Then the Lord said to him, "Now you Pharisees clean the outside of the cup and of the dish, but inside you are full of greed and wickedness. You fools! Did not the one who made the outside make the inside also? So give for alms those things that are within; and see, everything will be clean for you.

Luke 11:39–41

But woe to you Pharisees! For you tithe mint and rue and herbs of all kinds, and neglect justice and the love of God; it is these you ought to have practiced, without neglecting the others. Woe to you Pharisees! For you love to have the seat of honor in the synagogues and to be greeted with respect in the marketplaces. Woe to you! For you are like unmarked graves, and people walk over them without realizing it."

Luke 11:42–44

Then he told them a parable: "The land of a rich man produced abundantly. And he thought to himself, 'What should I do, for I have no place to store my crops?' Then he said, 'I will do this: I will pull down my barns and build larger ones, and there I will store all my grain and my goods. And I will say to

my soul, Soul, you have ample goods laid up
for many years; relax, eat, drink, be merry.' But
God said to him, 'You fool! This very night
your life is being demanded of you. And the
things you have prepared, whose will they be?'
So it is with those who store up treasures for
themselves but are not rich toward God."

Luke 12:16–21

Sell your possessions, and give alms. Make purses for yourselves that do not wear out, an unfailing treasure in heaven, where no thief comes near and no moth destroys. For where your treasure is, there your heart will be also.

Luke 12:33–34

Strive to enter through the narrow door; for many, I tell you, will try to enter and will not be able.

Luke 13:24

When once the owner of the house has got up and shut the door, and you begin to stand outside and to knock at the door, saying, "Lord, open to us," then in reply he will say to you, "I do not know where you come from." Then you will begin to say, "We ate and drank with you, and you taught in our streets." But he will say, "I do not know where you come from; go away from me, all you evildoers!"

Luke 13:25–27

Or what woman having ten silver coins, if she loses one of them, does not light a lamp, sweep the house, and search carefully until she finds it? When she has found it, she calls together her friends and neighbors, saying, "Rejoice with me, for I have found the coin that I had lost." Just so, I tell you, there is joy in the presence of the angels of God over one sinner who repents.

Luke 15:8–10

He also told this parable to some who trusted in themselves that they were righteous and regarded others with contempt: "Two men went up to the temple to pray, one a Pharisee and the other a tax collector. The Pharisee, standing by himself, was praying thus, 'God, I thank you that I am not like other people: thieves, rogues, adulterers, or even like this tax collector. I fast twice a week;

I give a tenth of all my income.' But the tax collector, standing far off, would not even look up to heaven, but was beating his breast and saying, 'God, be merciful to me, a sinner!' I tell you, this man went down to his home justified rather than the other; for all who exalt themselves will be humbled, but all who humble themselves will be exalted."

Luke 18:9–14

"For this son of mine was dead and is alive again; he was lost and is found!" And they began to celebrate.

Luke 15:24

PART FIVE

Consolation and Comfort

I will not leave you orphaned; I am coming to you. In a little while the world will no longer see me, but you will see me; because I live, you also will live. On that day you will know that I am in my Father, and you in me, and I in you.

John 14:18–20

Then the father said to him, "Son, you are always with me, and all that is mine is yours. But we had to celebrate and rejoice, because this brother of yours was dead and has come to life; he was lost and has been found."

Luke 15:31–32

As the Father has loved me, so I have loved you; abide in my love. If you keep my commandments, you will abide in my love, just as I have kept my Father's commandments and abide in his love. I have said these things to you so that my joy may be in you, and that your joy may be complete.

John 15:9–11

Everything that the Father gives me will come to me, and anyone who comes to me I will never drive away; for I have come down from heaven, not to do my own will, but the will of Him who sent me.

John 6:37–38

Do not be afraid, little flock, for it is your Father's good pleasure to give you the kingdom.

Luke 12:32

And the one who was seated on the throne said, "See, I am making all things new."

Revelation 21:5

The thief comes only to steal and kill and destroy. I came that they may have life, and have it abundantly.

John 10:10

Very truly, I tell you, if you ask anything of the Father in my name, He will give it to you. Until now you have not asked for anything in my name. Ask and you will receive, so that your joy may be complete.

John 16:23–24

I am among you as one who serves.

Luke 22:27

Those who belong to this age marry and are given in marriage; but those who are considered worthy of a place in that age and in the resurrection from the dead neither marry nor are given in marriage. Indeed they cannot die anymore, because they are like angels and are children of God, being children of the resurrection.

Luke 20:34–36

Now He is God not of the dead, but of the living; for to Him all of them are alive.

Luke 20:38

One of the criminals who were hanged there kept deriding him and saying, "Are you not the Messiah? Save yourself and us!" But the other rebuked him, saying, "Do you not fear God, since you are under the same sentence of condemnation? And we indeed have been condemned justly, for we are getting what we deserve for our deeds, but this man has done nothing wrong." Then he said, "Jesus, remember me when you come into your kingdom." He replied, "Truly I tell you, today you will be with me in Paradise."

Luke 23:39–43

I have said this to you, so that in me you may have peace. In the world you face persecution. But take courage; I have conquered the world!

John 16:33

While they were talking about this, Jesus himself stood among them and said to them, "Peace be with you."

Luke 24:36

They were startled and terrified, and thought that they were seeing a ghost. He said to them, "Why are you frightened, and why do doubts arise in your hearts? Look at my hands and my feet; see that it is I myself. Touch me and see; for a ghost does not have flesh and bones as you see that I have."

Luke 24:37–39

I am the bread of life. Whoever comes to me will never be hungry, and whoever believes in me will never be thirsty.

John 6:35

Go home to your friends, and tell them how much the Lord has done for you, and what mercy he has shown you.

Mark 5:19

Peace I leave with you; my peace I give to you. I do not give to you as the world gives. Do not let your hearts be troubled, and do not let them be afraid.

John 14:27

To everyone who conquers I will give some of the hidden manna, and I will give a white stone, and on the white stone is written a new name that no one knows except the one who receives it.

Revelation 2:17

My sheep hear my voice. I know them, and they follow me. I give them eternal life, and they will never perish. No one will snatch them out of my hand.

John 10:27–28

When I saw Him, I fell at his feet as though dead. But He placed His right hand on me, saying, "Do not be afraid; I am the first and the last, and the living one. I was dead, and see, I am alive forever and ever; and I have the keys of Death and of Hades."

Revelation 1:17–18

Blessed are those who mourn, for they will be comforted.

Matthew 5:4

Do not let your hearts be troubled. Believe in God, believe also in me.

John 14:1

But when they saw him walking on the sea, they thought it was a ghost and cried out; for they all saw him and were terrified. But immediately he spoke to them and said, "Take heart, it is I; do not be afraid." Then he got into the boat with them and the wind ceased.

Mark 6:49–51

Rejoice and be glad, for your reward is great in heaven, for in the same way they persecuted the prophets who were before you.

Matthew 5:12

Therefore I tell you, do not worry about your life, what you will eat or what you will drink, or about your body, what you will wear. Is not life more than food, and the body more than clothing? Look at the birds of the air; they neither sow nor reap nor gather into barns, and yet your heavenly Father feeds them. Are you not of more value than they? And can any of you by worrying add a single hour to your span of life? And why do you worry about clothing? Consider the lilies of the field, how they grow; they neither toil nor spin, yet I tell you, even Solomon in all his glory was not clothed like one of these. But if God so clothes the grass of the field, which is alive today and tomorrow is thrown into the oven, will he not much more clothe you—you of little faith? Therefore do not worry, saying, "What will we eat?" or "What will we drink?" or "What will we wear?"

Matthew 6:25–31

Truly I tell you, there is no one who has left house or brothers or sisters or mother or father or children or fields, for my sake and for the sake of the good news, who will not receive a hundredfold now in this age—houses, brothers and sisters, mothers and children, and fields, with persecutions—and in the age to come eternal life. But many who are first will be last, and the last will be first.

Mark 10:29–31

To the one who conquers I will give a place with me on my throne, just as I myself conquered and sat down with my Father on His throne.

Revelation 3:21

So do not worry about tomorrow, for tomorrow will bring worries of its own. Today's trouble is enough for today.

Matthew 6:34

Ask, and it will be given you; search, and you will find; knock, and the door will be opened for you. For everyone who asks receives, and everyone who searches finds, and for everyone who knocks, the door will be opened.

Matthew 7:7–8

So have no fear of them; for nothing is covered up that will not be uncovered, and nothing secret that will not become known. What I say to you in the dark, tell in the light; and what you hear whispered, proclaim from the housetops. Do not fear those who kill the body but cannot kill the soul; rather fear Him who can destroy both soul and body in hell. Are not two sparrows sold for a penny? Yet not one of them will fall to the ground apart from your Father. And even the hairs of your head are all counted. So do not be afraid; you are of more value than many sparrows.

Matthew 10:26–31

And Jesus answered him, "Blessed are you, Simon son of Jonah! For flesh and blood has not revealed this to you, but my Father in heaven. And I tell you, you are Peter, and on this rock I will build my church, and the gates of Hades will not prevail against it. I will give you the keys of the kingdom of heaven, and whatever you bind on earth will be bound in heaven, and whatever you loose on earth will be loosed in heaven."

Matthew 16:17–19

I have compassion for the crowd, because they have been with me now for three days and have nothing to eat; and I do not want to send them away hungry, for they might faint on the way.

Matthew 15:32

Those who find their life will lose it, and those who lose their life for my sake will find it.

Matthew 10:39

Take care that you do not despise one of these little ones; for, I tell you, in heaven their angels continually see the face of my Father in heaven. What do you think? If a shepherd has a hundred sheep, and one of them has gone astray, does he not leave the ninety-nine on the mountains and go in search of the one that went astray? And if he finds it, truly I tell you, he rejoices over it more than over the ninety-nine that never went astray. So it is not the will of your Father in heaven that one of these little ones should be lost.

Matthew 18:10–14

Again, truly I tell you, if two of you agree on earth about anything you ask, it will be done for you by my Father in heaven. For where two or three are gathered in my name, I am there among them.

Matthew 18:19–20

All authority in heaven and on earth has been given to me.

Matthew 28:18

And remember, I am with you always, to
the end of the age.

Matthew 28:20

The seventy returned with joy, saying, "Lord, in your name even the demons submit to us!" He said to them, "I watched Satan fall from heaven like a flash of lightning. See, I have given you authority to tread on snakes and scorpions, and over all the power of the enemy; and nothing will hurt you. Nevertheless, do not rejoice at this, that the spirits submit to you, but rejoice that your names are written in heaven."

Luke 10:17–20

And he said to them, "Suppose one of you has a friend, and you go to him at midnight and say to him, 'Friend, lend me three loaves of bread; for a friend of mine has arrived, and I have nothing to set before him.' And he answers from within, 'Do not bother me; the door has already been locked, and my children are with me in bed; I cannot get up and give you anything.' I tell you, even though he will not get up and give him anything because he is his friend, at least because of his persistence he will get up and give him whatever he needs."

Luke 11:5–8

Is there anyone among you who, if your child asks for a fish, will give a snake instead of a fish? Or if the child asks for an egg, will give a scorpion? If you then, who are evil, know how to give good gifts to your children, how much more will the heavenly Father give the Holy Spirit to those who ask Him!

Luke 11:11–13

PART SIX

Grace and Sanctification

For God so loved the world that He gave His only Son, so that everyone who believes in Him may not perish but may have eternal life.

John 3:16

The kingdom of God is not coming with things that can be observed; nor will they say, "Look, here it is!" or "There it is!" For, in fact, the kingdom of God is among you.

Luke 17:20–21

Then he told this parable: "A man had a fig tree planted in his vineyard; and he came looking for fruit on it and found none. So he said to the gardener, 'See here! For three years I have come looking for fruit on this fig tree, and still I find none. Cut it down! Why should it be wasting the soil?' He replied, 'Sir, let it alone for one more year, until I dig around it and put manure on it. If it bears fruit next year, well and good; but if not, you can cut it down.'"

Luke 13:6–9

Sanctify them in the truth; your word is truth. As you have sent me into the world, so I have sent them into the world. And for their sakes I sanctify myself, so that they also may be sanctified in truth.

John 17:17–19

So you also, when you have done all that you were ordered to do, say, "We are worthless slaves; we have done only what we ought to have done!"

Luke 17:10

I am the light of the world. Whoever follows me will never walk in darkness but will have the light of life.

John 8:12

You search the scriptures because you think that in them you have eternal life; and it is they that testify on my behalf. Yet you refuse to come to me to have life.

John 5:39–40

A Samaritan woman came to draw water, and Jesus said to her, "Give me a drink." The Samaritan woman said to him, "How is it that you, a Jew, ask a drink of me, a woman of Samaria?" Jesus answered her, "If you knew the gift of God, and who it is that is saying to you, 'Give me a drink,' you would have asked

Him, and He would have given you living water
… Everyone who drinks of this water will be
thirsty again, but those who drink of the water
that I will give them will never be thirsty. The
water that I will give will become in them a
spring of water gushing up to eternal life."

John 4:7–14

I am the living bread that came down from heaven. Whoever eats of this bread will live forever; and the bread that I will give for the life of the world is my flesh.

John 6:51

A sower went out to sow. And as he sowed, some seed fell on the path, and the birds came and ate it up. Other seed fell on rocky ground, where it did not have much soil, and it sprang up quickly, since it had no depth of soil. And when the sun rose, it was scorched; and since it had no root, it withered away. Other seed fell among thorns, and the thorns grew up and choked it, and it yielded no grain. Other seed fell into good soil and brought forth grain, growing up and increasing and yielding thirty and sixty and a hundredfold.

Mark 4:3–8

You are the light of the world. A city built on a hill cannot be hid.

Matthew 5:14

Very truly, I tell you, everyone who commits sin is a slave to sin. The slave does not have a permanent place in the household; the son has a place there forever. So if the Son makes you free, you will be free indeed.

John 8:34–36

Very truly, I tell you, whoever keeps my word will never see death.

John 8:51

Whoever welcomes one such child in my name welcomes me, and whoever welcomes me welcomes not me but the one who sent me.

Mark 9:37

I am the gate. Whoever enters by me will be saved, and will come in and go out and find pasture.

John 10:9

"Children, how hard it is to enter the kingdom of God! It is easier for a camel to go through the eye of a needle than for someone who is rich to enter the kingdom of God." They were greatly astounded and said to one another, "Then who can be saved?" Jesus looked at them and said, "For mortals it is impossible, but not for God; for God all things are possible."

Mark 10:24–27

Be perfect, therefore, as your heavenly Father is perfect.

Matthew 5:48

Indeed, God did not send the Son into the world to condemn the world, but in order that the world might be saved through him.

John 3:17

For the Son of Man came not to be served but to serve, and to give his life a ransom for many.

Mark 10:45

The words that I have spoken to you are spirit and life.

John 6:63

Why do you ask me about what is good? There is only one who is good. If you wish to enter into life, keep the commandments.

Matthew 19:17

But he replied to one of them, "Friend, I am doing you no wrong; did you not agree with me for the usual daily wage? Take what belongs to you and go; I choose to give to this last the same as I give to you. Am I not allowed to do what I choose with what belongs to me? Or are you envious because I am generous?" So the last will be first, and the first will be last.

Matthew 20:13–16

For many are called, but few are chosen.

Matthew 22:14

Give therefore to the emperor the things that are the emperor's, and to God the things that are God's.

Matthew 22:21

All who exalt themselves will be humbled, and all who humble themselves will be exalted.

Matthew 23:12

Well done, good and trustworthy slave; you have been trustworthy in a few things, I will put you in charge of many things; enter into the joy of your master.

Matthew 25:23

"A man was going down from Jerusalem to Jericho, and fell into the hands of robbers, who stripped him, beat him, and went away, leaving him half dead. Now by chance a priest was going down that road; and when he saw him, he passed by on the other side. So likewise a Levite, when he came to the place and saw him, passed by on the other side. But a Samaritan while traveling came near him; and when he saw him, he was moved with pity. He went to him and bandaged his wounds, having poured oil and wine on them. Then he put him on his own animal, brought him to an inn, and took care of him. The next day he took out two denarii, gave them to the innkeeper, and said, 'Take care of him; and when I come back, I will repay you whatever more you spend.' Which of these three, do you think, was a neighbor to the man who fell into the hands of the robbers?" He said, "The one who showed him mercy." Jesus said to him, "Go and do likewise."

Luke 10:30–37

When you are invited by someone to a wedding banquet, do not sit down at the place of honor, in case someone more distinguished than you has been invited by your host; and the host who invited both of you may come and say to you, "Give this person your place," and then in disgrace you would start to take the lowest place. But when

you are invited, go and sit down at the lowest
place, so that when your host comes, he may
say to you, "Friend, move up higher"; then
you will be honored in the presence of all
who sit at the table with you. For all who exalt
themselves will be humbled, and those who
humble themselves will be exalted.

Luke 14:8–11

He said also to the one who had invited him, "When you give a luncheon or a dinner, do not invite your friends or your brothers or your relatives or rich neighbors, in case they may invite you in return, and you would be repaid. But when you give a banquet, invite the poor, the crippled, the lame, and the blind. And you will be blessed, because they cannot repay you, for you will be repaid at the resurrection of the righteous."

Luke 14:12–14

PART SEVEN

Faith and Fulfillment

I am the resurrection and the life. Those who believe in me, even though they die, will live, and everyone who lives and believes in me will never die.

John 11:25–26

Those who believe in him are not condemned; but those who do not believe are condemned already, because they have not believed in the name of the only Son of God. And this is the judgment, that the light has come into the world, and people loved darkness rather than light because their deeds were evil. For all who do evil hate the light and do not come to the light, so that their deeds may not be exposed. But those who do what is true come to the light, so that it may be clearly seen that their deeds have been done in God.

John 3:18–21

Jesus answered, "Very truly, I tell you, no one can enter the kingdom of God without being born of water and Spirit. What is born of the flesh is flesh, and what is born of the Spirit is spirit. Do not be astonished that I said to you, 'You must be born from above.' The wind blows where it chooses, and you hear the sound of it, but you do not know where it comes from or where it goes. So it is with everyone who is born of the Spirit."

John 3: 5–8

Then Jesus was led up by the Spirit into the wilderness to be tempted by the devil. He fasted forty days and forty nights, and afterwards he was famished. The tempter came and said to him, "If you are the Son of God, command these stones to become loaves of bread." But he answered, "It is written, 'One does not live by bread alone, but by every word that comes from the mouth of God.'"

Matthew 4:1–4

I am the good shepherd. I know my own and my own know me, just as the Father knows me and I know the Father. And I lay down my life for the sheep. I have other sheep that do not belong to this fold. I must bring them also, and they will listen to my voice. So there will be one flock, one shepherd.

John 10:14–16

The kingdom of God is as if someone would scatter seed on the ground, and would sleep and rise night and day, and the seed would sprout and grow, he does not know how. The earth produces of itself, first the stalk, then the head, then the full grain in the head. But when the grain is ripe, at once he goes in with his sickle, because the harvest has come.

Mark 4:26–29

I can do nothing on my own. As I hear, I judge; and my judgment is just, because I seek to do not my own will but the will of him who sent me.

John 5:30

Blessed are the meek, for they will inherit the earth.

Matthew 5:5

Whoever believes in me believes not in me but in him who sent me. And whoever sees me sees him who sent me. I have come as light into the world, so that everyone who believes in me should not remain in the darkness.

John 12:44–46

With what can we compare the kingdom of God, or what parable will we use for it? It is like a mustard seed, which, when sown upon the ground, is the smallest of all the seeds on earth; yet when it is sown it grows up and becomes the greatest of all shrubs, and puts forth large branches, so that the birds of the air can make nests in its shade.

Mark 4:30–32

Believe me that I am in the Father and the Father is in me; but if you do not, then believe me because of the works themselves. Very truly, I tell you, the one who believes in me will also do the works that I do and, in fact, will do greater works than these, because I am going to the Father. I will do whatever you ask in my name, so that the Father may be glorified in the Son. If in my name you ask me for anything, I will do it.

John 14:11–14

Blessed are the poor in spirit, for theirs is the kingdom of heaven.

Matthew 5:3

A great windstorm arose, and the waves beat into the boat, so that the boat was already being swamped. But he was in the stern, asleep on the cushion; and they woke him up and said to him, "Teacher, do you not care that we are perishing?" He woke up and rebuked the wind, and said to the sea, "Peace!

Be still!" Then the wind ceased, and there was a dead calm. He said to them, "Why are you afraid? Have you still no faith?" And they were filled with great awe and said to one another, "Who then is this, that even the wind and the sea obey him?"

Mark 4:37–41

Daughter, your faith has made you well; go in peace, and be healed of your disease.

Mark 5:34

When you have lifted up the Son of Man, then you will realize that I am he, and that I do nothing on my own, but I speak these things as the Father instructed me. And the one who sent me is with me; he has not left me alone, for I always do what is pleasing to him.

John 8:28–29

Do not fear, only believe.

Mark 5:36

Blessed are the pure in heart, for they will see God.

Matthew 5:8

Have faith in God. Truly I tell you, if you say to this mountain, "Be taken up and thrown into the sea," and if you do not doubt in your heart, but believe that what you say will come to pass, it will be done for you. So I tell you, whatever you ask for in prayer, believe that you have received it, and it will be yours.

Mark 11:22–24

Be faithful until death, and I will give you the crown of life.

Revelation 2:10

Let anyone who is thirsty come to me, and let the one who believes in me drink. As the scripture has said, "Out of the believer's heart shall flow rivers of living water."

John 7:37–38

Truly I tell you, this poor widow has put in more than all those who are contributing to the treasury. For all of them have contributed out of their abundance; but she out of her poverty has put in everything she had, all she had to live on.

Mark 12:43–44

I came into this world for judgment so that those who do not see may see, and those who do see may become blind.

John 9:39

But strive first for the kingdom of God and his righteousness, and all these things will be given to you as well.

Matthew 6:33

Very truly, I tell you, no one can see the kingdom of God without being born from above.

John 3:3

Go and tell John what you have seen and heard: the blind receive their sight, the lame walk, the lepers are cleansed, the deaf hear, the dead are raised, the poor have good news brought to them. And blessed is anyone who takes no offense at me.

Luke 7:22–23

You know me, and you know where I am from. I have not come on my own. But the one who sent me is true, and you do not know him. I know him, because I am from him, and he sent me.

John 7:28–29

To everyone who conquers, I will give permission to eat from the tree of life that is in the paradise of God.

Revelation 2:7

I do not judge anyone who hears my words and does not keep them, for I came not to judge the world, but to save the world. The one who rejects me and does not receive my word has a judge; on the last day the word that I have spoken will serve as judge, for I have not spoken on my own, but the Father who sent me has himself given me a commandment about what to say and what to speak. And I know that his commandment is eternal life. What I speak, therefore, I speak just as the Father has told me.

John 12:47–50

Blessed are those who hunger and thirst for righteousness, for they will be filled.

Matthew 5:6

Then they said to him, "What must we do to perform the works of God?" Jesus answered them, "This is the work of God, that you believe in him whom he has sent."

John 6:28–9

This is indeed the will of my Father, that all who see the Son and believe in him may have eternal life; and I will raise them up on the last day.

John 6:40

Then he said to me, "It is done! I am the Alpha and the Omega, the beginning and the end. To the thirsty I will give water as a gift from the spring of the water of life. Those who conquer will inherit these things, and I will be their God and they will be my children."

Revelation 21:6–7

As you go, proclaim the good news, "The kingdom of heaven has come near."

Matthew 10:7

Whoever welcomes you welcomes me, and whoever welcomes me welcomes the one who sent me.

Matthew 10:40

Come to me, all you that are weary and are carrying heavy burdens, and I will give you rest. Take my yoke upon you, and learn from me; for I am gentle and humble in heart, and you will find rest for your souls. For my yoke is easy, and my burden is light.

Matthew 11:28–30

The kingdom of heaven may be compared to someone who sowed good seed in his field; but while everybody was asleep, an enemy came and sowed weeds among the wheat, and then went away. So when the plants came up and bore grain, then the weeds appeared as well. And the slaves of the householder came and said to him, "Master, did you not sow good seed in your field? Where, then, did these weeds come from?" He answered, "An enemy has done this." The slaves said to him, "Then do you want us to go and gather them?" But he replied, "No; for in gathering the weeds you would uproot the wheat along with them. Let both of them grow together until the harvest; and at harvest time I will tell the reapers, 'Collect the weeds first and bind them in bundles to be burned, but gather the wheat into my barn.'"

Matthew 13:24–30

The kingdom of heaven is like yeast that a woman took and mixed in with three measures of flour until all of it was leavened.

Matthew 13:33

The kingdom of heaven is like treasure hidden in a field, which someone found and hid; then in his joy he goes and sells all that he has and buys that field.

Matthew 13:44

Peter answered him, "Lord, if it is you, command me to come to you on the water." He said, "Come." So Peter got out of the boat, started walking on the water, and came toward Jesus. But when he noticed the strong wind, he became frightened, and beginning to sink, he cried out, "Lord, save me!" Jesus immediately reached out his hand and caught him, saying to him, "You of little faith, why did you doubt?" When they got into the boat, the wind ceased. And those in the boat worshiped him, saying, "Truly you are the Son of God."

Matthew 14:28–33

Again, the kingdom of heaven is like a merchant in search of fine pearls; on finding one pearl of great value, he went and sold all that he had and bought it.

Matthew 13:45–46

Let them alone; they are blind guides of the blind. And if one blind person guides another, both will fall into a pit.

Matthew 15:14

For the Son of Man is to come with his angels in the glory of his Father, and then he will repay everyone for what has been done.

Matthew 16:27

Whatever you ask for in prayer with faith, you will receive.

Matthew 21:22

A man had two sons; he went to the first and said, "Son, go and work in the vineyard today." He answered, "I will not"; but later he changed his mind and went. The father went to the second and said the same; and he answered, "I go, sir"; but he did not go. Which of the two did the will of his father?

Matthew 21:28–31

Heaven and earth will pass away, but my words will not pass away.

Matthew 24:35

Whoever listens to you listens to me, and whoever rejects you rejects me, and whoever rejects me rejects the one who sent me.

Luke 10:16

At that same hour Jesus rejoiced in the Holy Spirit and said, "I thank you, Father, Lord of heaven and earth, because you have hidden these things from the wise and the intelligent and have revealed them to infants; yes, Father, for such was your gracious will."

Luke 10:21

Jesus said to him, "Have you believed because you have seen me? Blessed are those who have not seen and yet have come to believe."

John 20:29

All things have been handed over to me by my Father; and no one knows who the Son is except the Father, or who the Father is except the Son and anyone to whom the Son chooses to reveal him.

Luke 10:22

If you had faith the size of a mustard seed, you could say to this mulberry tree, "Be uprooted and planted in the sea," and it would obey you.

Luke 17:6

A Note About the Compiler

Andrea Kirk Assaf has had the rare privilege of covering three pontificates in the span of a decade—the pontificates of John Paul II, Benedict XVI, and Francis. In 2002 she moved to Rome to write for *Inside the Vatican* magazine and several other Catholic and secular news outlets, covering World Youth Day in Toronto, the funeral of John Paul II, the election of Pope Benedict XVI, and now the popularity of the first successor of St. Peter from the New World, Pope Francis. Along with her editor-journalist-translator husband Tony Assaf and their four children, Andrea divides her days between the Eternal City of Rome and a rural homestead in Remus, Michigan.

Acknowledgments

Thanks are due to Helen Rochester at HarperCollins*Publishers* U.K. for assigning and guiding this project, to Tomás Valle, Matthew Smith, and Ulysa Girard for their creativity and good judgement in helping me select themes and quotes, and to Maya Assaf for diligently assisting me in copying passages from Scripture.

Reader's Journal

A Note on the Reader's Journal

The following pages of the reader's journal offer a space for reflection on the words of Jesus contained in this little book. In keeping with the thoughts in the opening note, these pages are organized to parallel the journey of a Christian as outlined in the selection of themes for Jesus' quotes. As we read through these quotes divided by theme and reflect upon their impact and relevance today, we can record ways in which we recognize the call of discipleship in our own lives, or how we find ourselves listening, watching, and remembering through the contemplation of these words. We can note the various trials and tribulations we face, praying and offering thanks for the comfort and consolation we have received. We can even express repentance by privately writing down our sins and then seeking forgiveness, not forgetting to make a note of the glimmers of grace and sanctification we receive along the way. Finally, in the faith and fulfillment section, we can copy down our creeds and favorite prayers for reference and recitation.

In this way, we can make of this small book a portable and continual retreat to use over the years on our journey through life, or for a particular time or occasion. The book could, of course, also be gifted to a loved one to mark a special occasion, with the reader's journal filled with notes, relevant quotes selected from each section, and blessings just for him or her.

The Call to Discipleship

The Call to Discipleship

The Call to Discipleship

The Call to Discipleship

The Call to Discipleship

The Call to Discipleship

The Call to Discipleship

Listen, Watch, Remember

Listen, Watch, Remember

Listen, Watch, Remember

Listen, Watch, Remember

Listen, Watch, Remember

Listen, Watch, Remember

Listen, Watch, Remember

Trial and Tribulation

Trial and Tribulation

Trial and Tribulation

Trial and Tribulation

Trial and Tribulation

Trial and Tribulation

Trial and Tribulation

Repentance and Forgiveness

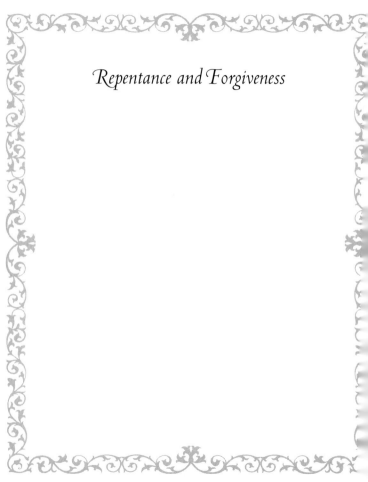

Repentance and Forgiveness

Repentance and Forgiveness

Repentance and Forgiveness

Repentance and Forgiveness

Repentance and Forgiveness

Repentance and Forgiveness

Consolation and Comfort

Consolation and Comfort

Consolation and Comfort

Consolation and Comfort

Consolation and Comfort

Consolation and Comfort

Consolation and Comfort

Grace and Sanctification

Grace and Sanctification

Grace and Sanctification

Grace and Sanctification

Grace and Sanctification

Grace and Sanctification

Grace and Sanctification

Faith and Fulfillment

Faith and Fulfillment

Faith and Fulfillment

Faith and Fulfillment

Faith and Fulfillment

Faith and Fulfillment

Faith and Fulfillment